The Gladiolus: Its History, Species and Cultivation

by John Lewis Childs
of Floral Park, New York

with an introduction by Roger Chambers

COVER CREDITS

Front Cover
Gladiolus Close Up by Calvin Yeung (Own work)
[CC BY-SA 3.0 (https://creativecommons.org/licenses/by-sa/3.0)]
or
[GFDL (http://www.gnu.org/copyleft/fdl.html)],
via Wikimedia Commons

Back Cover
Gladiolus decoratus 2 by Ton Rulkens from Mozambique
[CC BY-SA 2.0 (https://creativecommons.org/licenses/by-sa/2.0)],
via Wikimedia Commons

Research / Sources
Wikimedia Commons
www.Commons.Wikimedia.org

Many thanks to all the incredible photographers, artists,
researchers, and archivists who share their great work.

PLEASE NOTE :
As with all reprinted books of this age that are intended to perfectly reproduce the original edition,
considerable pains and effort had to be undertaken to correct fading and sometimes outright damage to
existing proofs of this title. At times, this task can be quite monumental, requiring an almost total
rebuilding of some pages from digital proofs of multiple copies. Despite this, imperfections still sometimes
exist in the final proof and may detract slightly from the visual appearance of the text.

DISCLAIMER :
Due to the age of this book, some methods or practices may have been deemed unsafe or
unacceptable in the interim years. In utilizing the information herein, you do so at your
own risk. We republish antiquarian books without judgment or revisionism, solely
for their historical and cultural importance, and for educational purposes.

Self Reliance Books

Get more historic titles on animal and stock breeding, gardening and old fashioned skills by visiting us at:

http://selfreliancebooks.blogspot.com/

introduction

I am very pleased to present to you another wonderful old book on horticulture – *The Gladiolus : Its History, Species and Cultivation*. It was written by John Lewis Childs, and first published in 1893, making it well over a century old.

At *Self Reliance Books* we endeavor to bring you the best in antiquarian and out-of-print books. With the recent up-swing in interest in all subjects about growing various things, we are re-publishing some great old titles on horticulture and agricuture. This short little book is one of those titles.

The book features topics like Hybrid Gladiolus, The Lemoine Hybrids, Cultivation of the Gladiolus, Gladiolus from Seed, and more.

Although this little old book has just 38 pages, and is short and sweet, it is still a valuable addition to your horticulture library for flower growers in general, and for Gladiolus enthusiasts in particular.

~ Roger Chambers

State of Jefferson, December 2017

1

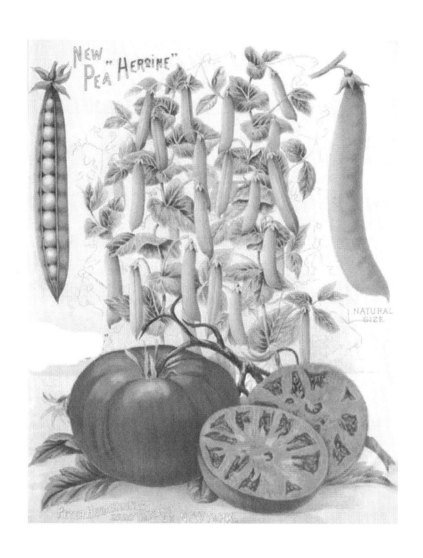

THE GLADIOLUS.

THE history of the Gladiolus is, in many respects, a remarkable one. Not one of the species, of which there are more than sixty, that go to make up the genus, are found under cultivation, excepting in botanical collections. Yet they are strangely beautiful, but the desire for forms and colors other than the natural ones, which is common with all plants has driven the species from our gardens, only to return in good time.

The Gladiolus is one of the most important genera of the order *Iridaceæ* in which is found, the Crocus, Iris, Tigridia, Tritoma, Ixia, and several others, which are very generally cultivated, without any marked change through hybridization. With but few exceptions, the species that make up this genus, are mostly natives of the Cape of Good Hope. A few species are found in the South of Europe; a few also come from Natal.

The species are remarkable for their ease of culture, grace of habit, singular forms of flowers and intense coloring, ranging from the most vivid scarlet to pure white; from clear rose to almost pure yellow, and bright purple; in many of the species the colors are singularly blended. The habits of the species, contrast as strangely as their colors. In height they vary from one to four feet; some are delicate and light, others robust and strong, with constitutions adapted to any climate excepting the more frigid.

Like the introduction of most other plants, the Gladiolus has an uncertain history. It seems strange that, notwithstanding the grace and rare beauty of many of the species, and the marvellous improvement made in the flower by hybridization within the past fifty years, it should have been in the English garden for more than 300 years without claiming any special attention.

Gerarde, in his quaint old Herbal, 1597, speaks of several kinds he had cultivated in his time, and that were then common. Ray, who was more of a florist and naturalist, writes in 1660 of the Gladiolus or corn flag, as of no great esteem, and only consents to the admission of them in his garden because they come in a season (June and July) when there are not many other flowers.

Miller, in his dictionary of plants, 1757, mentions and describes about thirty species and as many more varieties, showing the Gladiolus was then better known and more highly appreciated, and that considerable attention was paid to the growing of them from seed. But very little is said or known of any attempts, at that time, at cross-fertilization for the improvement of the race. *G. Cardinalis* flowered in a Kensington Nursery in 1790, and created considerable of a sensation. While it is classed as a species, it was, by many, considered a variety. Whatever may have been its origin, whither it is a species, which is highly probable, or a seedling, it matters but little in comparison to the important fact of its being one of the parents of the now popular class known as the hybrids of Gandavensis, itself a hybrid.

Loudon, one of the most far-seeing and comprehensive minds that was ever devoted to horticulture, failed to see in the Gladiolus the capabilities for development it so richly possessed. In his encyclopædia of plants, he only numerates thirty species, the same number that Miller noticed in his Dictionary of Gardening, some fifty years before. But Loudon failed to appreciate the work being done at that time by a contemporary Dean Herbert, the great authority on bulbs, who had then made some valuable crosses between the species, the result of which was a number of varieties which were considered of great merit at that time, because of the great improvement they showed over the species.

For the Gladiolus of the present day we are indebted to the late Louis Von Houtte, of Ghent, Belgium, whose intelligent labors as a hybridist, gave us the well known hybrids of Gandavensis, which, later, were so wonderfully developed, and distributed by Mon. Souchet, of Fontainblau, France.

Owing to the remarkable hybrids that have been produced, but few of the species are now found under cultivation, notwithstanding the fact that some of them possess the most wonderful beauty, as well as remarkable characteristics. The more important of the species we shall describe not only because of their intrinsic merits, but because of their importance, as parents of the now popular forms.

Gladiolus Alatus, (*The Winged Gladiolus.*) This singular little bulb was first introduced by Thunberge, from the Cape in 1795—but soon lost, and again introduced in 1827. It is classed with the hardy species, and, through a small flower, is a remarkably handsome one. Like most of the so-called hardy species, the bulbs are very small, not as large as a small Crocus.

G. Albidus, (*The White Gladiolus.*) This species is white in a relative sense only, but is as near an approach to it as any of the species. It is a native of the Cape, introduced in 1794. The flowers are small and delicate. Not in general cultivation.

G. Algoensis, (*The Algoa Bay Gladiolus.*) This species belongs to the viper division of Gladiolus. (See *G. Viperatus.*) It is one of the more hardy kinds, but in this climate must have the protection of a frame, as much to protect against water, as against cold. It must also have free air and sunshine. It was introduced in 1824 from the East coast of South Africa. The flowers have but little of interest to other than the botanist.

G. Blandus, (*The Fair Gladiolus.*) This species is closely allied to *G. Carneus*, but with white flowers, the lower divisions of which are stained with oval spots of red. It is a handsome species, the flower stems grow from two to three feet high, and produce from eight to ten flowers, ranked alternately on each side, a form not now considered desirable.

G. B. Campanulatus, (*The Bell-shaped Gladiolus.*) This was formerly considered a species, but now a variety of *G. Blandus*. It is a very handsome flower, but singularly ill-named, as its flowers are less bell-shaped than most of the other species. The color is lilac, with a red stain on each of the lower divisions.

G. Brachyandrus, (*Short-stemmed Gladiolus.*) This species was introduced from Tropical Africa in 1879. Like all the species it is not under general cultivation. Its flowers are a clear pale scarlet, produced on short spikes, with eight to ten flowers each.

G. Byzantinus. This species is a native of Turkey and is quite distinct. The flowers are self-colored reddish purple, and are particularly desirable as they appear much earlier than the hybrid forms. This species may be said to be perfectly hardy, and when once planted in the border may remain several years without separating, as it produces so few off-sets that it requires a long time to become troublesome from crowding. There are two or three varieties of the species, varying only in their shades of color. The bulbs are small, and should be planted in Autumn, and given a free, open situation, as they require full sunshine for a perfect development of their flowers.

G. Cardinalis, (*The Scarlet Gladiolus.*) This is unquestionably the most showy of the species, and the leading one under cultivation, previous to the appearance of the hybrid forms. The flower stem, when grown in favorable situations, is very tall, fully four feet high, and generally sends out near the top five or six branches, each bearing from six to eight flowers, color a brillant scarlet, with a white diamond-shaped spot on each division. The bulbs may be planted in the spring, like the common forms, but they will succeed far better if planted in October, in a dry soil, and protected with a slight covering of leaves. It does not increase rapidly, and can remain undisturbed for a number of years. It is a native of the Cape, and was introduced in 1789.

This species has been of great value to the hybridist, as it crosses more freely than any other ; this fact has made it the leading parent of our present types. It, crossed with *G. Blandus*, gave us many of the light varieties that were so popular just previous to the introduction of the Gandavensis section. But for its flowers being borne all on one side of the stem, it would still occupy a prominent place in the garden.

G. Carneus, (*The Flesh Colored Gladiolus.*) This is a handsome, strong growing plant, of rather a dwarf habit, rarely reaching three feet in height. The flowers are very large, flesh-colored with brilliant Carmine diamond-shaped spots on the lower divisions. From its free-flowering habit, and the large size of the flowers, it makes a showy plant in the garden. Like most of the species, the bulbs should be planted in the Autumn, and carefully protected. They come into flower fully a month earlier than our hybrid forms.

G. Cochleatus, (*The Spoon-tipped Gladiolus.*) A curious species, with a very slender stem sometimes nearly two feet long. It is what is called a white-flowered sort ; the three upper segments are about half the size of the lower ones, and more erect ; they are stained with a red feathery mark ; the lower segments are white, and the central one, spoon-shaped. The fact of its being a green house variety, as it flowers in February, prevents its general cultivation.

G. Colvillei, although a hybrid sort, the result of a cross between *G. Concolor* and *G. Cardinalis*, is usually classed with the species, because of a distinct character or habit. It is a very dwarf growing plant, rarely exceeding one and a half feet high. The flowers are a bright scarlet with purple markings, and when opening have a delicious fragrance. It is specially adapted to pot culture. There are now some fine hybrids of G. Colvillei which are particularly fine for winter blooming.

G. C. Alba, a variety of the above, is of the same general character as the above, but the flowers are the nearest pure white of any of the family. It has been largely grown by the florists for cut flowers, and is popularly known as " The Bride."

G. Communis, (*Common.*) This species, which is a native of the South of France, has been longer under cultivation than any of the species, and is included in the seedsmen's catalogues with the hardy bulbs. Relatively, it is such, but it will rarely endure the rigors of our winter without protection. Of this species there are several varieties, rose, purple and white flowered. They are all of very dwarf and slender habit, and come into flower early in June, which makes them desirable. Compared with our present-types, they are not showy, yet they are well worth a place among our hardy plants, as they can be grown in the border with slight protection. The bulbs should be taken up and separated as often as once in three years, as they produce such an immense quantity of offsets that they will, as Parkinson said in 1629, "Choke and pester the garden rather than be an ornament to it."

G. Concolor, (*The One-colored Gladiolus.*) This is a desirable species, or has been, because of its color, which is of a clear bright yellow ; the form of the flowers are more bell-shaped than any other of the species ;

WINTER BLOOMING GLADIOLI.

the great projection of the mid-rib making the section appear, when cut, in the form of the Greek cross. They produce but few flowers, and those on one side of the stem. In the day-time, the flowers have no fragrance, but in the evening they diffuse an odor like that of the common pink.

G. Cuspidatus (*The Sharp-pointed Gladiolus.*) This is one of the most remarkable species of the genus, from the great length and wavy appearance of the petals. The flowers, which are produced in May or June, are cream-colored, but the lower divisions are marked with a very rich purple spot. This mark is much larger and more brilliant in some flowers than in others. This species has been very useful in cross fertilization; it is a native of the Cape, introduced in 1795.

G. Eudalis, (*The Edible Gladiolus.*) This species was found in the interior of South Africa. The flower has no beauty, being white, slightly stained with pink and yellow : the petals being very narrow, and much curled they look withered as soon as they expand. The bulbs are roasted like chestnuts, which they closely resemble in taste, and are a favorite food of the natives. This species requires greenhouse culture.

G. Fasciatus, (*The Swathed Gladiolus.*) This is a very pretty. dwarf species, the stem seldom growing above six inches high, and never exceeding a foot. The flowers are of a delicate pink color, the petals have waved margins, the three lower ones having a dark crimson streak down each. This makes a beautiful plant when grown in a pot, as the stem is greatly branched; with a little care the plant can be made to grow in the form of a little bush, completely covered with flowers ; a beautiful window-plant.

G. Gracilis, (*The Slender Gladiolus.*) This is one of the least desirable of all the Gladiolus, it has not a point to recommend its cultivation. Its flowers are few, of poor shape and color and without fragrance.

G. Hastatus, (*Halbert-shaped Gladiolus.*) It has been questioned as to whether this is a species, or a variety of *G. Blandus ;* so closely does it resemble the latter that it is safe to class them as one species.

G. Hirsutus, (*The Hairy Gladiolus.*) This species has been classed with *G. brevifolius,* although they are entirely distinct. The flowers are large, rose colored, and like most of the species, they appear on one side of the stem only ; they are peculiar, because of their deep red margins, and for their being quite hairy. This plant varies much according to the soil in which it is planted. Sometimes it will not be more than one foot high, in other situations it will be more than four feet. It must be planted in the Autumn, and be amply protected against frost. The native habitat is unknown , it was introduced into England from Holland in 1795.

G. Papilio, (*The Butterfly-flowered Gladiolus.*) This very strange and beautiful bulb first flowered at Kew in 1866, having been introduced from the Cape by their collector, Mr. Arnot. The flower is conspicuous because of its remarkable colors and markings. It is described as follows: " It attains the height of three feet ; leaves sword-shaped ; spike a foot long, many-flowered ; flowers one to two inches apart, sub-campanulate, expanding an inch and a half ; upper segments pale purple, with a faint dash of yellow ; lower lobes with broad deep purple band, beyond which is a band of gold, the margin pale purple."

G. Psittacinus (*The Parrot Gladiolus.*) This interesting species is a native of the south-east coast of Africa, being found near Port Natal. In a dry soil it may be said to be perfectly hardy. To the casual observer the flowers possess but little interest , although large and showy, the colors are so strangely blended they fail to please other than the eye of the botanist and hybridist who have developed from them, as one of the parents, those forms now so highly esteemed. In the open ground the flower stalks reach the height of four feet, and several are produced from each bulb.

G. Pendibundus, (*The blush-flowered Gladiolus.*) We class this with the species, because it is not now listed with the recent hybrid forms, although it is a cross between *G. Cardinalis* and *G. Blandus.* In habit of growth, in its delicate, light flowers, gracefully arranged, it is a far more beautiful plant than those under general cultivation. As it flowers early, the bulbs must be planted in à dry soil, and be thoroughly protected against frost.

G. Purpures Auratus, (*Purple and Golden.*) This species is a native of Natal, and was introduced in 1872. It is a delicate plant of a branching, straggling habit , the flowers are more cup-shaped than others of the species, pale yellow with very bold blotches of rosy-purple on the lower

II

GLADIOLUS PURPUREA AURATUS.

d.visions. For combination of color they outrival the most gorgeous colors of the Orchids. This species is particularly valuable, because of its being the parent of the popular class known as the Lamoine Hybrids, of which full reference will be made in another place.

G. Quartinianus. A somewhat dull yellow flowered variety with most of the petals more or less streaked with red. It is a native of Tropical Africa, and was first found in Abyssinia by Mr. Quartin Dillon, after whom it has been named. It is only to be found in botanical collections.

G. Ramosus, (*The branching Gladiolus.*) There exists considerable doubt as to whether this is a species or a hybrid form. It was introduced from Holland in 1836 and claimed to have come from the Cape of Good Hope. Whichever it may be, whether a species or a class, it is unquestionably of the greatest importance for garden ornament. In the size and beauty of its flowers it yields the palm to none, and on account of its peculiarly branching habit it may be considered the most ornamental. In favorable situations the flower stems will grow five feet high and produce a succession of flowers from June until August. The flowers are very large, well opened, and of good shape. Color, rosy-blush, with heavy carmine stains on the three lower divisions. The leaves are proportionately large and handsome, and the whole plant forms a magnificent object when given plenty of room for its development. The bulbs should be planted in the Fall, in a dry, sandy loam, and the bed protected from frost by a liberal mulching.

The Dutch claim to have found several varieties at the Cape from which they have procured a large number of cross-breeds, all partaking of the same general character, differing only in the colors of the flowers.

G. Recurvus, (*The Recurved or Violet-scented Gladiolus.*) This species has some very peculiar characteristics, differing in many respects from all others, not only in its color, which is a beautiful violet tinged with yellow, and its fragrance which resembles both that of the Violet and the Oris root, but by the sheath which rises from the bulb and envelops the case of the stem. This sheath is white, mottled with a purplish brown, and it is as glossy as the finest porcelain, which it greatly resembles. Each bulb sends up three leaves and a stem about two feet high, with a flower-spike of from two to five flowers. When the flowers first expand they will be found, if closely examined, to be yellow, so closely dotted over with very small violet-blue spots as to look quite blue at a distance; and in this state the flowers look quite beautiful. It is quite likely the near approach to blue we find in some of the hybrid forms, has its parentage in this species. Like others of the Cape species this should be planted in the fall and amply protected against both freezing and water, as either will cause it to perish. Seedlings without cross-fertilization, from this species are found to be much earlier, and never fail to produce flowers each season.

G. Saundersi. This fine species was sent to Mr. Saunders, Raystead, Eng., by his collector, Mr. Thomas Cooper, from South Africa, and named in his honor. In many respects this is the most remarkable species that goes to make up this noble genus. There appears in each species some peculiarity of special interest. In this it is the immense size of the flowers, some of which are six inches across; together with their intense scarlet-color and white throat, spotted with crimson. The form of this flower differs from all others, in the immense size of the lower divisions, which is just the reverse of all the genus. The nearest approach to this, of any of the species, is that of *G. Psittacinus*. While the species are remarkable for the display they make, they are still more remarkable in their progeny, being the direct parent of Max. Leichlien's new type, now known as *G. Childsi*, of which more mention will be made under the head of Hybrid Gladiolus.

G. Segetum. This species is closely allied to *G. Communis*, differing only in the arrangement of its flowers, and in their color which is a clear rose. It is a native of the south of Europe, and has been in cultivation since 1596.

G. Suaveolens, (*Sweet-scented Gladiolus.*) This is a singular little species, and but little known. The flowers are quite fragrant, of a pale-yellow or straw color, dotted in the upper part with red spots. It is most suitable for pots, as its curious markings would not be noticed in the open ground.

G. Tristis, (*The Melancholy-looking Gladiolus.*) This was one of the

GLADIOLUS SAUNDERSI.

first of the species sent from the Cape to England, and flowered at Chelsey in 1745. It was described by Linnæus, and named *Tristis*, because of its sombre appearance. The flowers are cream-color, with a green stripe running through each petal ; the three upper petals have the stripe dotted with purplish-red ; the outside of the petals are feathered with the same color. It requires the same treatment as all the Cape species.

G. Versicolor, (*The Changeable Gladiolus*.) A handsome species, the flowers of which somewhat resemble those of the Parrot-Gladiolus. This species was introduced in 1794, and it flowers in June. It emits a pleasing fragrance in the evening ; its flower-stems are short, each usually gives four flowers. The name *Versicolor* appears to allude to the slight change in color which is visible at sunset.

Gladiolus Viperatus, (*The Viper Gladiolus*.) The name " Viperatus " was given this very singular plant from the resemblance of part of its flower to the head of a viper when raised and hissing, as if just preparing to bite. The flowers are of a greenish gray, with livid and brown stripes ; and they are exceedingly fragrant. This species is a native of the Cape of Good Hope, whence it was first sent to England about 1794. It is now rarely met in collections.

There are many more species which might be noticed, but these mentioned include all that are practically distinct. The space given these is not warranted by the position they occupy in the garden, but rather for the position they should occupy there. In the cultivation of flowers the popular taste appears to be away from natural forms, rather than toward them. In this respect the botanist is antagonistic, in his selection, to the florist. In thwarting the purposes of nature, new forms and strange combinations of color is the result, but whether they are more beautiful is a question that individual taste alone must decide, our work being simply descriptive.

HYBRID GLADIOLUS.

The history and description of the Gladiolus is important, as it shows what changes have been made by hybridization, cultivation and selection. In no branch of floriculture has the skill, the zeal, and the perseverance of the hybridizer been more liberally rewarded, than in the crossing of the various species of Gladiolus, and the development of the forms produced. Several separate and distinct classes, with almost an unlimited number of varieties of each have been produced. In no class of plants has the changes been more marked than in this. The varieties in many cases, bear but little resemblance to the parents. Forms have been materially changed ; colors separated, so that nearly all the primitive ones found, even in the smallest proportion in the species, have become selfs in the varieties ; markings have become changed ; delicate stripes have been superceded by the bold colors found in some of the blotches, so conspicuous in some of the forms. Sharp, pointed petals have given place to round, symmetrical ones. Flowers of any desired form or color, compactly arranged on a long spike, itself hidden, has superceded the straggling, one-sided arrangement so conspicuous in most of the species. The number of flowers on a spike has been materially increased, and the time of flowering has kindly changed to suit our convenience, as well as our necessities. Delicate forms have been replaced by strong ones ; transient flowers have been succeeded by more enduring ones. In short, the species have readily changed their essential characters, as regards form, size and color, and have adapted themselves to the dictates of art more readily than any other class of plants.

The first, as well as the most important class produced, were the so called Hybrids of Gandavensis, itself a Hybrid and the parent of an immense array of beautiful forms.

16

The hybridization of any popular species, when it is attended with so little labor in proportion to results produced, as in this class, is speedily carried on to an extent which render characteristic distinctions indefinable, and, perhaps, the introduction of numberless names which necessarily arise from such circumstances is to be regretted, as occasioning difficulty and labor beyond what most cultivators are willing to submit to. For the purposes of sale, however, and, also, to enable the producer to perpetuate very desirable sorts, it is essential that every variety produced that is worthy of being disseminated should have a distinctive name. But in this respect the past few years has witnessed a marked and important change. Where a dozen distinct forms or varieties was considered a valuable collection, they no longer satisfy, and hundreds are planted instead. Classes have taken the places of names, and masses under colors are planted, instead of an individual bearing a distinctive name.

GANDAVENSIS HYBRIDS.

HYBRIDS OF GANDAVENSIS.

As we have before stated, this was the first important class that was developed by hybridization and cross-fertilization, and, in the great variety of florist's flowers, if we except the rose, no class contained so many named varieties. For a long number of years, even to the present day, the origin of *G. Gandavensis* was in doubt, and a question for dispute. Why, we never could understand, as we have the word of one of the most prominent horticulturists in the world, the late Louis Van Houtte, whose word was authority on anything pertaining to the history of plants, that it was a seedling raised in the garden of the Duke of Avenburg, a celebrated amateur in Ghent, and that it was the result of a cross between the species *Cardinalis* and *Psittacinus*. This should have been regarded a settlement of the question in dispute. Not so, however, for the late Hon. and Rev. Wm. Herbert, an acknowledged authority on bulbs, said Mr. Van Houtte was in error, for after repeated attempts to hybridize the two species named, he, Mr. Herbert, could not succeed, consequently it could not be done, and what Mr. Van Houtte said he knew, from his own personal knowledge, had been done was a mistake ; and all the English authorities agree with Mr. Herbert that the origin of *G. Gandavensis* is obscure.

There is no question, however, as to the fact that to *G. Gandavensis* we are indebted for the development of this family of plants, that has been carried on for more than fifty years, without as yet reaching the limit of its possibilities. This cross has completely overcome the difficulty experienced in getting the many species to hybridize, as all the varieties of *Gandavensis*, cross with the species, so that new types are constantly appearing, and each has some mark of superiority, either in form or color, not possessed by the parent. Why crosses should have this effect is one ot the mysteries, past finding out ; if it is to stimulate a love for the beautiful in floral forms, and to show there is no limit to development, the object is attained.　It is a common mistake to call our many varieties *hybrids*, which are a direct cross between species.　In the Gladiolus, the first cross is but the commencement of that development in the flower that has given it a world-wide reputation, and it is one of the most interesting features in the cultivation of this flower, that every cross between well-known varieties tends in almost every case to improve, not only the beauty of the flower but the vigor of the plant.　This principal is as plainly marked in the new types we shall mention as with the hybrids of *Gandavensis*.

LEMOINE HYBRIDS.

THE LEMOINE HYBRIDS.

(*G. hybridus Lemoineanus.*) The introduction of this class gave new life to the interest already manifested in the cultivation of the Gladiolus; it opened a new door into the world of plants, in which there was a rich field for the hybridist to investigate and develop. This fine hybrid Gladiolus was the result of a cross between G. purpureo-auratus, a true species and a native of Natal, and G. Gandavensis, the origin of which we have already stated, made by that eminent horticulturist, M. Lemoine, of Nancy, France, and justly bears his name. This new type, which grows from three to four feet high, partakes in a striking degree of the character of both parents, with a marked tendency towards the perennial character of G. purpureo auratus. It is more nearly hardy than the Gandavensis parent, and the bulblets do not cling so closely to the new bulb, but are pushed away by slender root-like stems. These bulblets are larger than those of the Gandavensis section, and not unfrequently flower the first season; they are, moreover, liable to lose their vitality by getting dry. The seeds seem to partake of the same nature. We have had these produce flowers the same year they are planted, which we have never known others to do.

The type is of robust growth, with foliage of a rich green color. Its flowers, which are about the size of the ordinary garden Gladiolus, are arranged closely on the spike, which is much branching, like the Ramosus section, each branch, as well as the main spike, is more than a foot in length. The three upper petals, which are broad, are of a creamy white color, the lowermost one is conspicuous for its heavy blotch of rich, deep purplish crimson, the other two petals are the same color, excepting about one-half inch of the tips, which is clear yellow, giving the flower a striking appearance. Improvement has marked the way of this class, as with the first hybrids, and the list of varieties produced is a long one, and the colors as varied as with the former class. There is, however, the same bold markings on the lower petals, the same graceful habit with the plant, and its flowers, because of this drooping habit, do not make so much display in the garden as those of the other classes. A close observation is necessary to reveal the real beauty of this class.

GLADIOLUS CHILDSI

GLADIOLUS CHILDSI.

A new strain of wonderful magnificence which was first introduced to cultivation this year by Mr. John Lewis Childs.

HISTORY.—This wonderful class of hybrids was produced by Herr Max Leichtlin, of Germany, the most noted horticulturist in the world, and is the result of crossing and re-crossing G. Saundersoni with G. Gandavensis. From his hands they passed to Monsieur G. LeBeuf, Mayor of Argentieul, France, who cultivated and propagated them for several years, until the entire stock was imported to the United States in 1887. In 1891 they came into Mr. Childs' possession at the purchase price of $20,000. The stock now consists of about 400 distinct varieties, which will be duly named, and about 500,000 mixtures and seedlings of blooming size. Six sorts were named and offered this year, and seven more have been named for offering next year.

Max Leichtlin says: "I was struck with the broad, open form of the flowers of G. Saundersi, and having carefully selected the best among the Gandavensis section, I repeatedly crossed the Saundersi; the final result is the present race of Gladioli (Childsi), distinguished by their exceptionally wide open flowers and their beautiful colors."

G. LeBeuf says: "I can truthfully say that I have cultivated this Gladioli to the greatest of my satisfaction. In appearance and color it is royal and unsurpassed. Its coloring is distinct in every detail, varying from a self color to all the delicate shades."

DESCRIPTION.—It is difficult to describe flowers of such varied and peculiar beauty as these Gladiolus, and it can only be done by a comparison with other sorts. They are much stronger and more vigorous than others, the growth being exceedingly rank, and the foliage dark, healthy green. They are very tall and erect, often standing four

24

or five feet high with spikes of bloom over two feet in length. They branch freely, in most cases each stem producing four spikes of bloom. The flowers are of great substance and of gigantic size, frequently 7 to 9 inches across. The form of both the flower and the spike is perfection itself, and they last in bloom a long time before fading, owing to their great substance and vigor, but the most remarkable feature is their coloring. Orchids cannot surpass them in varied and delicate shades, markings and blendings. Every color known among Gladiolus is represented, and many never before seen, particularly blues, smokey-grays and purple-blacks, all having beautifully mottled and spotted throats, made up of white, crimson, pink, yellow, etc., and in this peculiar net-work of charming spots and colors lies one of its special points of unsurpassed beauty. The flowers are more beautifully colored than Lemoine's Hybrids, and much larger than Gandavensis. Even the beautiful flowers of the weak-growing Nanciaenus can not compare with the regal beauty, size or colors of this class.

NANCIAENUS HYBRIDS.

These were first offered in France a few years ago. Like Childsi, they are hybrids of Saundersi, and the flowers are of good size and finely colored, yet inferior to Childsi in this respect. In growth they are very weak, frail and unhealthy, as compared with Gandavensis, Lemoine, and Childsi Hybrids.

CULTIVATION OF THE GLADIOLUS.

There is no class of flowers that will thrive better or with less care, under varied circumstances than the Gladiolus. It dislikes a stiff clayey soil but will thrive well in almost any other ; its preference being for one of a moist, sandy nature, or light loam. They succeed best on sod ground, with but little manure, and that well rotted. A soil that had been made very rich for a previous crop, is well suited to it. Successive plantings on the same soil should be avoided ; change the locality of the bed so as not to return to the spot for three years. In small gardens, sod ground is out of the question, and a rotation of crops is not always convenient. We only state the best conditions, then let necessity govern the planting. The Gladiolus will bear close planting, four inches apart each way will afford sufficient room for a perfect development of the flower. The bulbs should be covered according to the character of the soil; if very light, cover them with five inches of soil ; if very heavy, one inch will be sufficient.

The first plantings should be made as early as the soil can be got in good working order, and for succession, plant every two weeks until the first of July, or, where there is no danger from frost before the middle of November, the last planting can be made as late as the middle of July. For late planting, the largest bulbs should always be reserved, as the smaller ones, which produce quite as good, if not better flowers, are apt to dry out, and lose their vitality by keeping too long out of ground. When the bulbs are taken up, they should be kept in a dry dark room, or cellar, where they can be kept as cool as possible, providing the temperature does not fall below the freezing point.

Increase of desirable sorts is effected by the small bulbs or bulblets that form at the base of the new bulb ; these are produced in greater or less quantities, for some cause or causes we do not understand. Some varieties will produce on an average a hundred per year, others scarcely any ;

this will, in a great measure, account for marked difference in the cost of the named sorts ; it will also account for the rapid increase of some of the more common kinds, and the sudden disappearance of those greatly prized. All the varieties are short-lived unless they produce bulblets. In many of our named sorts old bulbs will not produce good flowers, if, indeed, they produce any, consequently the bulblets of all desirable sorts should be saved and planted each spring ; at least a sufficient number for a required stock.

The question is frequently asked, " Do the varieties sport, or return to the type, or do the white and the yellow grounds put on a scarlet ? " To all these interrogatories we usually say, " it is our opinion they do not," at the same time the phenomena of plant life is but little understood, and so strange in many respects, that it is not safe to be positive about anything related to it. That they do change is, by many, earnestly believed. An enthusiastic amateur once said to the writer: " The first year or two after I made up my collection it was superb, in fact, the varieties were the best I could obtain ; now they are not worth growing, all red, or dull colors ; what is the cause ? " We replied, and our experience has confirmed the opinion : " The light colors have less vitality, as a rule than the dark ones, consequently they do not as rapidly reproduce, and like all other delicate forms they soon pass away. On the contrary, most of the older varieties are nearer the type of hardy, robust parent and possess healthy, strong constitutions, and increase with great rapidity. Hence the accumulation of the one, and the loss of the other.

We have planted small bulbs of the variety Brenchleyensis, and when taken up in the fall have taken from a single bulb more than two hundred well-ripened bulblets. From a bulb of Shakespeare, of the same size, a bulb that never flowers well excepting from young bulbs, would not get, on an average, a dozen. This shows that the rare kinds die out, and the more common ones multiply so rapidly that quantity is kept in stock at the expense of quality.

The bulblets may be sown in early spring in any convenient out of the way place in the garden. If in good soil they will, with proper care in cultivation, nearly all flower the second year. The first season they require but little room, make the drills the width of a common garden hoe, two inches deep ; sow the bulblets so close that they will nearly touch each other, and they will do much better than if more scattered. Take up as soon as the tops begin to wither, or as soon as the new bulb begins to turn brown, break off the tops, and put away in the same manner as recommended for the large bulbs. Plant these out the coming spring as early as possible, as because of their small size they are apt to loose vitality by being kept too long out of ground.

GLADIOLUS FROM SEED.

The raising of Gladiolus from seed is as easy a task as that of growing the most common of garden vegetables. The only secret, or mystery is that one can, with so little trouble, and relatively no expense, produce flowers that will give such intense satisfaction and pleasure. Prepare bed in spring, the same as for any hardy annual ; the soil should be finely prepared and moderately rich; sow the seed in drills, say, ten inches apart; cover to the depth of one inch. Use the hoe carefully so as not to disturb the roots, but keep entirely free from weeds, Take up the bulbs soon after the first frost or before if they show by the drying up of the tops the bulbs are ripe, and keep them during winter, the same as the older bulbs. If the season has been favorable for their growth a large proportion of them will flower the coming season.

We know of no pleasure in gardening that is equal to the growing of this class of plants from seed. The certainty of getting some remarkably fine varieties, is well balanced by some that are decidedly uninteresting, with an occasional one that has all the characteristics of the species so far removed from the present ideal of a perfect flower that the astonishment at the result is a sufficient recompense for the labor employed. Upon the whole, when the proper care is exercised in the selection of seed, a marked improvement may be expected. The fact that the best rarely flower first, will tend to create in the amateur a warm and watchful interest.

A pertinent and common question is, how to obtain the best seed? This is the result of selection. Save your seed from such varieties as are the most pleasing; the amateur to be the sole judge of that matter. Always bear in mind the first requisite is a sound constitution; no matter how beautiful the flower may be, if the plant that produced it is delicate, seedlings from it will lack vitality. A strong growing plant, with flowers of good form and color, is the one to produce seed for future use.

Cross-fertilization is the method to be employed, with a view to improvement, but it is a delicate work, and not always successful. This may be because it has been imperfectly done, but few understand the practice in detail, and the good results obtained, may, after all be the result of accident. The finest seedlings ever produced in this country were accidentals; they came from seed gathered from the best flowering plants, and such only should be saved, and sowed in the same manner as that which had received all possible care as to cross-fertilization. All that were worthy of name came in this way, while those produced by cross-fertilization failed to give a plant worthy of perpetuation.